STARTERS PLACES

Mexico

Macdonald Educational

About Starters Places

Starters Places provide an entertaining and informative introduction for young children to various countries and their national characteristics.

The vocabulary is controlled for reading by young children, and about 90 per cent of the words in the book should be familiar to young readers.

Each book contains material for further activities and research, such as an easy reference map, a table of simple facts, a project, a dictionary and an index.

Teachers and experts have been consulted on the content and accuracy of the books.

Illustrated by: William Hewison

Written and planned by: Sandie Oram

Managing editor: Su Swallow

Production: Stephen Pawley, Rosemary Bishop

Art consultant: Geoffrey Dickinson of *Punch*

Reading consultant: Donald Moyle, author of *The Teaching of Reading* and senior lecturer in education at Edge Hill College of Education

Chairman, teacher advisory panel: F. F. Blackwell, Director, Primary Extension Programme, National Council for Educational Technology; general inspector for schools (primary), London Borough of Croydon

Teacher panel: Loveday Harmer, Lynda Snowdon, Joy West, Enid Wilkinson

Series devised by: Peter Usborne

Colour reproduction by
Colourcraftsmen Limited

SBN 356 04056 9
Made and printed in Great Britain
by Purnell & Sons Limited
Paulton, Somerset

Filmset by
Layton-Sun Limited

First published 1972 by
Macdonald and Company
(Publishers) Limited
St. Giles House
49-50 Poland Street
London W1

This is a party in Mexico.
These children are opening the piñata.
They throw sticks at it.
When it tears, sweets fall out.

Acapulco is warm and sunny,
even at Christmas.
Many tourists come here on holiday.
Sometimes they buy Mexican sombreros.

There are very high cliffs in Acapulco.
Divers jump off them into the sea.
The tourists watch them.

These Mexicans are fishing in the sea.
Some dive for conch shells.
Others catch turtles.

Tourists come to Mexico to fish.
Sometimes they see dolphins.
They watch the dolphins.
Dolphins are very clever animals.

Here are some boats.
They take people to see
the flower gardens near Mexico City.
Thousands of flowers grow on the lake.

These people are cutting henequen.
Sometimes this plant is called agave.
It is used to make a drink called tequila.

This factory makes string and rope.
They are made from the inside
of the henequen plant.
The strings are twisted into rope.

Here is a silver mine.
Silver is found in the ground.
Men mine the silver.
They take it away in trucks.

This silversmith is making jewellery.
He beats the silver.
He shapes it into necklaces and rings.

Many Indians live in Mexico.
Some make pottery to sell.
This Indian girl is painting a plate.
She will sell it in the market.

Here is a Mexican market.
There are many things to buy.
Most people are buying food.

Mexicans often eat tortillas.
Tortillas are a kind of pancake.
Sometimes they are rolled round
meat and vegetables.

Here is a Mexican dance.
The men stamp their feet.
The girls whirl round.

The Indians have their own dances.
This dance is in a festival.

These new buildings are in Mexico City.
They have huge pictures on them.
Some of the pictures
are old Indian designs.

Popocatapetl is a volcano.
Sometimes it sends out smoke.
Popocatapetl means smoking mountain.

Some parts of Mexico are jungle.
There are many wild animals there.
These people are hunting wild boars.

This Mexican boy has a pet.
It is an iguana.
An iguana is a kind of lizard.
Some people eat iguanas.

Mexico long ago

Long ago the Maya lived in Mexico.
Some were astrologers.
They knew all about the stars.

The Aztecs lived in Mexico too.
They played a kind of basketball.
They had a ball court in the temple.
The players hit the ball through the ring.

Men from Spain discovered Mexico.
They met Montezuma, the Aztec king.
Montezuma gave them treasure.

Many Spaniards stayed in Mexico.
They became farmers.
They lived in haciendas.
They were the first cowboys.

You will need:

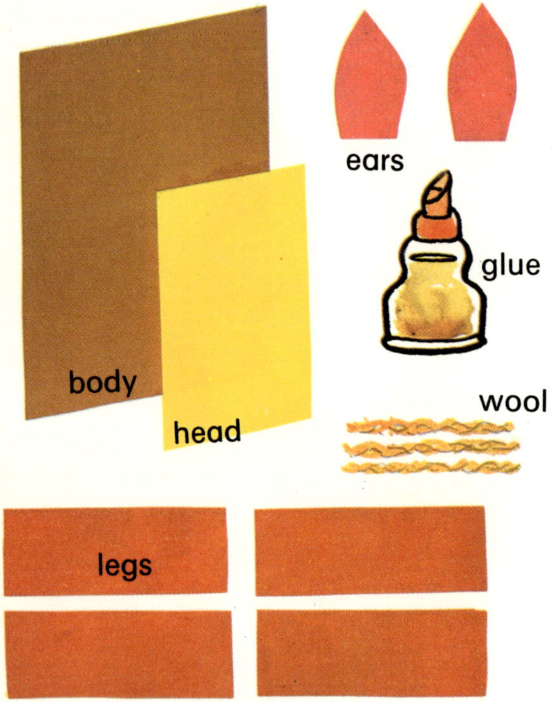

1. Roll up the body and the head into tubes and glue them.

2. Cut holes for the legs. Roll up the legs tightly and push through the holes.

3. Glue the head to the body. Stick on the ears and tail.

See if you can make a Mexican donkey.
You can make it in paper or card.

Starter's **Mexican** words

I	is	yo
you	is	tu
friend	is	amigo
hello	is	quihubo
goodbye	is	adios
I play	is	juego
I eat	is	como
good	is	bueno
bad	is	malo
thank you	is	gracias

Here are some Mexican words.
They are like Spanish words,
because Spaniards came to live in Mexico.

Index